Blessing Our Goodbyes

Blessing Our Goodbyes

A Gentle Guide to Being with the Dying and Preparing for Your Own Death

KATHIE QUINLAN

RESOURCE *Publications* · Eugene, Oregon

BLESSING OUR GOODBYES
A Gentle Guide to Being with the Dying and Preparing for Your
Own Death

Biblical passages are from the Bible in Basic English, ed., by S. H.
Hooke and published by Cambridge Press in 1941 (revised 1965). The
BBE is in the public domain and can be quoted without restriction.

Resource Publications
An Imprint of Wipf and Stock Publishers
199 W. 8th Ave., Suite 3
Eugene, OR 97401

www.wipfandstock.com

ISBN 13: 978-1-61097-313-7

Manufactured in the U.S.A.

To my dearest Bill, with me all the way

Contents

Foreword

WHEN I first met Kathie Quinlan, I wondered if she might be a saint. Her soft, high-pitched voice and strong sense of spirituality made her appear almost ethereal. Yet shortly thereafter I learned that beneath this cherubic exterior lay a tireless and passionate advocate both for her own patients as well as for other patients who were dying without the benefit of hospice care. In Rochester, she developed a two bed hospice residence called Isaiah House that became known for its willingness to take some of our community's poorest and most challenging patients. Kathie has been very frustrated by and vocal about our culture's persistent denial of our mortality, and the terrible consequences of depriving patients and families of much of the meaning and connection that is possible in the last phase of the life cycle if we could somehow find the courage to face it squarely. She has always been both a romantic and a realist about hospice. Her attention to the details of each patient's story of illness, their relationships before and after becoming sick, and their spiritual journey more often than not allowed her and her team to find what healing might be possible for each patient and family going through this process.

In her wonderful new book, *Blessing Our Goodbyes*, we learn initially about the personal losses that led Kathie to her life's work of caring for the dying. She also shares a wide range of her patients' stories. Some of these stories were of very accomplished individuals with tightly connected families that led them naturally to an acceptance of death and a kind of life closure that we all might hope for and find meaningful. At the other end of the spectrum (and this in many ways is the "specialty" of Isaiah House) were lives that had been tormented and fractured, and relationships that were severely damaged before the patient became terminally ill, where she and her team struggled to find what kind of closure and meaning was possible. We learn from this wider range of human experience that dying is filled with possibilities big and small, but there is no set formula. Yet Kathie shares what has worked for her, and in doing so gives us ideas and inspiration about how to proceed as caregivers with the most difficult cases as well as within our own lives. The players in these dramas include the patient and family, but also the patient's other caregivers and friends as well as the hospice personnel.

For those of us who for better or worse happen to be human, facing these issues including our own mortality at some point become core parts of our lives (though largely ignored or denied by most of us most of the time). Those of you who have found yourself unsure about what to say or what to do when confronted with a family member or friend or patient who is dying will get some gentle but definite guidance from Kathie in this book. She teaches us it usually begins with a kind, caring, listening presence, and a commitment to be with and respond to the patient all the way through the illness until the patient's death no matter what unfolds, and then on to the bereavement period for the family left behind. In the last chapter, Kathie also chides us and guides us to begin to prepare for our own mortality. Whether we are current caregivers or if we are contemplating our own eventual futures, we would all do well to consider the advice and guidance of this gentle, yet ferocious clinician.

TIMOTHY QUILL, MD

Professor of Medicine, Psychiatry, and Medical Humanities
University of Rochester School of Medicine and Dentistry
Rochester, New York

Acknowledgments

MY STORIES could never have been told had Isaiah House not continued "to be" these past twenty-four years. With all my heart, I thank my dear nurse friends who, with beautiful hospice-hearts and in a variety of ways over many years, have selflessly shared their compassionate gifts; the hundreds of loving volunteer caregivers—our greatest resource and blessing; all those who in countless ways have faithfully supported the mission of this home for the dying and the exceptional palliative care and hospice professionals in our community from whom I've learned so much.

My gratitude also to my cherished friend Arlene Helget, who worked steadfastly beside me as administrator for those first twenty years; to Cathy Fanslow, a most gifted hospice nurse whose insightful and gentle teachings twenty-five years ago have guided my efforts ever since; and to Fr. James Brady Callan, who bravely blessed the dream, making possible all that followed.

A heartfelt thanks to my precious family, including among others, my husband Bill, our dear daughters Beth and Dorothy, their husbands, and our 7 delightful grandchildren, who believe in the power of story and for whom this will be part of my legacy. And most of all, I am deeply and lovingly indebted to our dear daughter Linda and her husband Dave, for without their encouragement, guidance, and unfailing support, this book would never have been written.

Introduction

How daunting a task this book seemed to be when I first began. Yet how could I not write about the dying, for those dear hearts with whom I spent their last days have been my wisest of teachers. Perhaps their very human, often poignant, stories, which have long lingered with me, were waiting to be told so the value of their lessons could be shared with others. For it is through these stories that their lessons come to life. And so, with a head and heart full of such stories, I begin.

In the early to mid 60's, my husband Bill and I endured the untimely and devastating loss of two of our cherished five children. Both suffered a rare degenerative central nervous system disease about which little was known—at that time, it didn't even have a name. Virginia, our third little girl, died eighteen days after her first birthday, and Michael, our only son, just before his. How these precious little ones changed our lives, never again to be the same. One of the most treasured lessons we all learned was to live just one day at a time. Really, that was the only way we could live during those two agonizing years—watching, waiting, hoping for another day and then another. Both of our children died at home—in our own little hospice long before I was aware of the concept.

Throughout those times of holding fast and letting go, times of such tender losses, I began to feel a tugging at my

1

heart, a desire to become a nurse, specifically to care for the dying. I had often pondered the meaning of the saying, "God writes straight with crooked lines,"[1] Gradually its implication was becoming clearer. At the time, I was a part-time speech pathologist, anticipating many more years of mothering. Our first two little girls, Linda and Beth, were later joined by a dear adopted baby sister, Dorothy. Any inclination toward a nursing career would have to wait.

In 1978, my beloved father died of cancer. During the months of Dad's illness, and especially as I participated in his care, my desire for nursing began to nudge me more persistently. It was also during this time that I began to read Elisabeth Kubler-Ross's books on death and dying. This wise and wonderful woman graced my life and truly helped me through this painful time. Her words gave me the courage to say what I wouldn't have said before and to love more deeply. But also, she was leading me beyond, though I didn't realize this at the time. Later, I came to see that my father's dying, rather than his death, had the greater impact upon me. Those days with him had been an exquisite time of grieving, reminiscing, and letting go (though ever so reluctantly). Looking back, I see that they had planted in me an awareness of how such days of saying goodbye could be for others.

In the weeks following my father's death, memories of Virginia and Michael flooded my heart and began to take on new meaning. The "crooked lines" were becoming even straighter. Memories of painful events that had earlier made little sense were now filled with new understanding and purpose. The nudge was no longer gentle. As I pondered those experiences of aching loss, the missing

1. Ancient Portuguese proverb.

of what might have been—what should have been—I was brought to a moment of decision. With my family's loving confidence and enduring support, I entered nursing school at mid-life. During the five years of hospital nursing that followed my graduation in 1981, I continued to be drawn to the bedside of those who were dying. However, it was both disturbing and frustrating to me that in the hurried, cure-focused, acute care setting, the special needs of the dying were not easily met. There must be another way. Actually, at that time, more formal, certified hospice efforts did exist in Rochester. A health care agency offered skilled professional support to those wishing to die at home. Also, in a dedicated area within a nursing facility, special end-of-life care was provided. Still, some of us wondered if it were possible to approach this need less formally.

As it turns out, there was. In 1984, a unique and innovative concept for caring for the dying was introduced to Rochester: Mount Carmel House. Founded by a devout and loving couple, Rose and Raoul Grassi, and staffed primarily by volunteers, it offered compassionate, end-of-life care to two people at a time within a home-like setting. How grateful I have always been for this beautiful idea. It intrigued me. Two years earlier, our family had begun attending Corpus Christi Church, a revived and vibrant urban faith community led at that time by Fr. James Callan—a remarkable and faith-filled visionary person. Four outreach ministries had already blossomed with his blessing: a neighborhood health center, an outreach to the homeless, a prison ministry, and a child care center. Might it be possible to add another? Thankfully, it was. With Fr. Jim's guidance and support, and the unbelievably generous gifts of time, talent, and treasure by many others over the following three years, my dream of a home for the dying was realized in August 1987.

Isaiah House, a gracious old city home built in 1914, is what I have often called an "ordinary extraordinary" house. Its outside resembles many of the surrounding neighborhood homes. Yet upon entering, one senses a serenity and peace that is almost palpable. And with its soft-colored walls, comfortable furniture, flowers and plants, and special wall hangings, each conveying its own story, Isaiah House looks and feels like a home. It is within this atmosphere that the final journey of each dying person is regarded with reverence and unconditional love.

In the backyard, to everyone's delight, there is a beautiful meditation garden modeled after those found near English country cottages. Appreciating that those who care for the dying have a special need for the soothing balance offered by nature, two professional gardeners designed and, assisted by others, created a sacred space. In our earliest years, a little girl gazed longingly at the garden from our pantry window. "Oh," she said. "It looks like the Secret Garden" and, indeed, it does. So many tears have watered that glorious garden, and so many joyful moments have occurred there too. It is a gift to all who gaze upon it, an extension of the healing grace within the house.

You may be wondering how our house was named. In the prophet Isaiah's Book of Consolation found in the Bible are many hopeful and comforting passages. How perfectly they seemed to lend themselves to the spirit, the mission of our gentle ministry to the dying. Hence, the name Isaiah House was chosen. Several of the passages found a place in our brochure, among them "Comfort, give comfort to my people, says your God."[2] And this has always been our hallmark.

From the beginning, Isaiah House has had a small, salaried professional staff and a dedicated group of many trained volunteer caregivers. The House offers a residence for two people at a time who have irreversible illnesses and have been medically determined to be within the last three months of their lives. Loving hospitality and comfort care are given by volunteers in cooperation with a home health agency and each resident's physician. Preference for admission is given to those people who have diminished economic or psychosocial resources or those who, for a variety of reasons, are unable to remain in their own homes. Supported by donations, Isaiah House charges no fees. And so it continues, now in its twenty-fourth year. My twenty years as director have ended, yet I remain involved in end-of-life education for it is a part of my heart. Gratefully, the years following the opening of Isaiah House have seen the emergence of many other "little houses," both within and far beyond the Rochester community. This informal movement has been marked by the extraordinary generosity and compassion of hundreds of kindred spirits—yet another way of caring for the dying.

Over and over again, our cadre of compassionate caregivers quietly, unassumingly, and ever so tenderly minister to, wait with, and say goodbye to our residents. And in those countless vigil times, something quite wondrous happens. To the extent we have been open to the grace of these moments, we have better learned to face, even to embrace, our own mortality . . . to recognize that death is a natural

2. Isa 40:1.

part of our lives and a most unifying human experience. Being with the dying has taught us to live more fully, more freely, willing to take risks in those areas of our lives that have the greatest meaning, to have a heightened awareness of all that surrounds us and deeper insights into all that is within us. We have learned to live not only in the day, but in the moment, the moment we are in, to be open to and welcome whatever may come in that moment.

Our wise and wonderful teachers, the dying, have taught us well. Our work with them has been in a classroom like no other. It is from this extraordinary house and the many dear hearts within it that I will draw many of my stories.

A Change of Heart

Coming to View Life and Death Differently

*"Death is not extinguishing the light.
It is putting out the lamp because the dawn has come."*

—Rabindranath Tagore

THESE GENTLE words of the poet Tagore convey an image of serenity and peace. Tragically, our modern American society has dealt far less kindly, even defiantly, with death—often considering it an option (it isn't) and choosing to resist it at all cost. Our health care system is in chaos, and unceasing debates over end-of-life issues and concerns continue to be frustrating and disconcerting. Injudicious uses of technology, fueled by our denial of death, often serve not only to prolong but to dehumanize the dying process, stripping it of the sensitive and sacred respect it so rightly deserves. Conversely, the purposeful hastening of death by physician-assisted suicide gains support.

One thing is quite certain: our death will come. Much anguish would be spared, both for individuals and society, if each of us could come to terms with this anticipated, natural, and momentous event in our lives and allow death to come in its own time and in our own way. Death is the ending to which we all are born, the ultimate and most universal human experience beyond our birth. We know neither the hour nor the day, but at some point each of us will be in the throes of its mystery and majesty, its power and its pathos. Death has the remarkable ability to equalize; in that moment, we are all the same.

However, for so very many people, death remains a forbidden topic, its discussion not easily embraced. Most other societies in our world are more accepting of the reality of mortality, and they view Americans as rather peculiar for their reluctance to do the same. We even shun the word *die* as we employ euphemisms to describe the "dreaded event." Words and phrases, such as "passed," "pass away (on, over)," and "expire" are increasingly part of our vernacular. (My library card and my driver's license "expire," and I can re-new them both). Not long ago, I heard a TV news reporter refer to someone's "terminal event." Why is the word "die" so very troubling to say, to hear, and to think about? I find this avoidance perplexing.

Unfortunately, we live in a youth and beauty-obsessed culture in which images of youthfulness and vigor reign supreme. Shuddering at the first sign of wrinkles or sagging features, we hasten to erase them. Why do we hesitate to be ourselves *as we are*? So often, I've been drawn to the authenticity of the dying. It is truly humbling to be with people who show no falseness, no pretense, no façade. Rather, they are quite simply, beautifully themselves. If only we could live our lives this way!

The costly and sometimes dangerous efforts to thwart the signs of aging sadly seem to imply a denial of this very natural life progression. Certainly there are challenges to be met as we age, some of them quite considerable. But aren't there challenges in other seasons of our lives as well? Think back to earlier struggles you have confronted, difficulties you overcame, achievements you may have accomplished. Remember the satisfaction you felt. Might we not bring the fruits of our labors, the lessons of our life experiences, to guide us through these later challenges?

In his lovely book, *Anam Cara* (a book of Celtic wisdom), John O'Donohue suggests that "if you can come to see aging not as the demise of your body but as the harvest of your soul, you will learn that aging can be a time of great strength, poise, and confidence."[1] This "harvest season" of our lives presents a most remarkable opportunity for self-discovery, fulfillment, and promise. Why are we so hesitant, even fearful, to embrace this fruitful time?

Such musings about words and their implications have consumed many moments of my life. The word "holistic" has been among my favorites. Not only does it suggest a beautiful directive for caregiving but for living as well. Imagine how different our world would be if we regarded one another, as does holism, in each of our dimensions: physical, social, emotional, and spiritual. Our ability to really listen comes to mind. How often we hear someone toss into the air a "how are you" but hurry on without waiting for an answer? A wise adage suggests that we not ask a question if we are not willing to hear the answer.

Consider the frantic pace of our lives. So often when we are in a hurry we miss wonderful opportunities to truly

1. John O'Donohue, *Anam Cara* (New York: Clift Street Books, 1997), 167.

"be with" someone, to really connect. Julia Lane, in her article "Care of the Human Spirit," has defined the spirit as "a fragile vessel holding the essence of who we are. It is a sacred place."[2] This is such a lovely image of that exquisite dimension of our personhood that is so often overlooked. What if we became sensitive to each other's hearts and histories—to those fragile vessels within, seeking out their stories and listening without judgment? Because we often don't, how many stories have never been spoken or heard.

Our personal and powerful experiences are woven into the fabric of our lives, the content of our hearts. We cannot separate ourselves from them. Consider for a moment that we are no strangers to loss. Surely among our many stories are memories of loss, their impact ranging from devastation to disappointment—the life-changing loss of a child, a spouse, a parent, a sibling, a friend, a pet; significant, life-altering diminishments in our health and our abilities; the loss of a job with its accompanying worries and regrets. The list is endless! Couldn't these "little deaths" be preparing us for that ultimate loss, the relinquishing of our spirit at the moment of our death? Haven't they been teaching us all along the way? John O'Donohue writes:

> In the underside of life there is the presence of our death. If you really live your life to the full, death will never have power over you. It will never seem like a destructive, negative event. It can become, for you, the moment of release into the deepest treasures of your own nature. It can be your full entry into the temple of your soul. If you are able

2. Julia Lane, "Care of the Human Spirit," *Journal of Professional Nursing* 3 (1987): 333.

to let go of things, you learn to die spiritually in little ways during your life. When you learn to let go of things, a greater generosity, openness, and breath comes into your life. Imagine this letting go multiplied a thousand times at the moment of our death. That release can bring you to a completely new divine belonging.[3]

We ought to savor each moment, to live fully, deeply, passionately within it. *Carpe diem*, seize the day. You will never have it again. Admittedly, it takes much practice and discipline to live this way. It seems not to come easily, given our tendency to dwell on an unchangeable past or worry about an uncertain future. Not only do we squander much of our thinking time, but we also miss some of the wonderfully surprising moments right before our eyes. My own life has been blessed with many such moments, and very likely yours has too.

We live in perilous times. Our terror-threatened, war-torn, weary world is affecting how we relate to and interact with each other, how we trust or mistrust, what we believe or refuse to believe. We are feeling very fragile and vulnerable, and we certainly don't like feeling this way. If ever there was a time to live in the moment, it is now. We are also called to be mindful of our death, our constant companion. It is always with us, watching, waiting. Unfortunately, so many are choosing simply to ignore death and hence remain unprepared for its eventual reality. This is reflected in the troubling statistic that most Americans have *not* completed their Advance Directives—the Living Will and Health Care

---

3. O'Donohue, *Anam Cara*, 218.

Proxy—and therefore forfeit the ability to document their own wishes for treatment at life's ending.

Throughout my years working with the dying and their families, I've come to appreciate that the dying process is poorly understood and, consequently, often feared. This is very apparent in persistent, futile efforts to defy death at all cost. Noteworthy progress has been made in birthing education over the past forty or fifty years, while reflection on end-of-life considerations lags far behind. This is intriguing for there are so many parallels between the process of birthing and that of dying. Yet if more people acquired an understanding of the dying process, wouldn't their anxiety be eased? Hundreds of individuals—the dying, their families, and our caregivers—have found their experiences at Isaiah House to be transforming. I believe others could be similarly blessed!

I do not wish to romanticize death. I fully acknowledge its heartbreaking anguish. That cannot nor should not be ignored. Still, quite possibly, that anguish could be softened by accurate, sensitive support and guidance. Again and again, I found myself reflecting back on my teachers, the dying themselves. Could I perhaps be a voice for them in conveying lessons they taught me? Admittedly, minds are difficult to change, but not impossible. Since death's most profound and tender implications rest within our hearts, I hope to bring about a change of heart as well.

And so this book, this little offering, is drawn from countless bedsides where I have watched, waited, and learned. I am so deeply indebted to all those dear hearts. Among them was Roland, who came to Isaiah House soon after it opened in 1987. Born in Jamaica, he had lived many years in England. We loved his charming accent, a blending of his two countries. For six weeks, he delighted us with his grace and gentle humor. We were impressed by his openness in discussing his approaching death, his readiness to embrace it: "I'm going home . . . I'm going home to my Lord." Each day of that sixth week, he grandly repeated the phrase, "I'm going home to my Lord." On a bright, sunny autumn morning, as I opened the window blinds in his room, I said to him, "Roland, you didn't think there would be a new day for you, did you?" He replied, "Oh, no dear. There will always be a new day. Even if I wasn't here, someone else would see it." He died peacefully two days later at 6:00 a.m., as a new day was dawning, a day that someone else would see.

Roland's wisdom left such a mark on all of us who had grown to love him. In the following pages, I offer more stories to inspire and inform you as they have so many others. Hopefully, the word death may no longer be unthinkable.

". . . there is purposefulness in life when we no longer fear death."

—Anonymous

2

Getting There

The Unfolding of the Dying Process

"I don't know . . . I've never done it before."

M Y MOTHER'S voice, like her spirit, never seemed to age. In so many ways, she was perpetually young at heart. With joy and gratitude, we celebrated her 90th birthday. Mom was radiant and delighted in every moment of the festivities. While blessed with a keen, inquisitive, and energetic mind, she had bravely endured several serious assaults to her health. These included open heart surgery, a stroke and, twice, a hip fracture. The last Monday of August 2001, following rehabilitation for her second fracture, my two sisters and I were able to bring her back to her lovely apartment. She had so longed to be home. We planned to take turns spending the night and support her continuing recovery. By midweek, however, we began to notice an unsettling decline in her physical condition. As I waited with Mom at the doctor's office on Wednesday, she asked me, "Do you think this is the beginning of the end?" By Friday, everything had changed. I will never forget the moment, seemingly frozen in time, when I knelt by her recliner and asked, "Mom, do you think you might be dying?' (I already

14

thought that she was). And her reply? "I don't know. I've never done it before."

Mom's decisive intent not to return to the hospital clearly guided our efforts in the coming hours. Our only brother and sister-in-law arrived from the Midwest late that Friday evening just in time to have one last brief conversation with Mom for her ability to respond was quickly slipping away. We children remained steadfastly by her side, tenderly caring for her needs. Throughout the long hours of Saturday, so many people who loved her came to say goodbye to "Nana." Knowing she was no longer responsive, we assured everyone that she could hear their precious voices. Shared memories, messages of endearment, a song or two, tearful goodbyes all accompanied her journey throughout those long hours. It was truly a gift day as hearts were touched in both directions. Our vigil ended on Sunday at mid-afternoon as our beloved mother, surrounded still by her dear ones, was able to relinquish her spirit in the sacred moment of her death. It has been said that a good death is self-defined, and hers certainly was. And that also was a gift—to her and to us.

* * *

Serious life-threatening illness and the dying process render a most painful impact upon the hearts and lives of all involved. For the patient, and unique to this time, are several very special, very specific needs. Awareness of these needs can be so reassuring to the patient and immensely helpful to those surrounding him—a light of understanding shining on the fear and apprehension that often swirl about at such times.

While it is true that some choose to die alone, it is helpful to know that the fear of being alone is very real, very frightening for many. This does not mean that someone must be with the dying person every minute. Indeed, private, quiet times are a precious necessity for the dying. However, it is often a good idea to assure the person that she/he will not be left all alone. Long ago, as my father was dying of cancer, he frequently and confidently recalled the doctor's appointment when he and my mother were told that nothing further could be done to stop his advancing cancer. A young physician gently touched his arm and said, "Don't worry. We're not going to abandon you." Dad found much comfort in those reassuring words during the remaining days of his illness, and he quoted them frequently. We could call the hospice home care agency with our questions and concerns at any time. Skilled and caring professionals would be responsive, and his concerns would definitely not be ignored. In all the ways that mattered, he would not be alone. Dad died peacefully at home, surrounded by his family and his beloved Dalmatian, who had kept a steady vigil beneath the bed throughout the day.

The fear of abandonment is very real. In dying, one ventures into unknown territory. The understanding support of those one loves, trusts, and respects is critical. The person may feel sad and isolated if family members and friends appear to be distancing themselves, not knowing what to say or how to be with someone who is dying. At the same time, families frequently feel overwhelmed and helpless by what they perceive is ahead for them all. Their feelings should not be ignored.

Years ago, I was astonished when a young woman for whom I was caring admitted that she felt she had disappointed her physician because of her failure to respond to the prescribed treatment. Oh, my! Indeed, the treatment had failed her, but she had done nothing wrong. Unfortunately, many physicians, uncomfortable with death themselves and regarding it as a failing on their part, distance themselves from their dying patients—an act that can feel like abandonment to them. This is especially sad when a patient and physician have shared a long history. Such a view not only dishonors that privileged relationship, it also deprives the physician of the enriching experience of accompanying the patient on this journey.

* * *

Dying is part of living. We willingly share our experience of living all our lives. Why should this special time—the time of our dying—be different? Death has been called the final stage of growth. This implies change and spiritual enrichment. Regrettably, both the patient and those of us who watch and wait sometimes fail to allow this final stage its fullest dimension. Perhaps it is because we are afraid to be reminded of the impermanence of life, afraid to enter into a union with hearts that are breaking. It is true that some of us are unable to speak comfortably of this profound and meaningful part of our lives. Some people by nature are less communicative than others. They may prefer not to share their dying time. Of course, this wish should be respected. But for many others, there is a sincere desire for self-expression, far beyond trivial comments about the weather. How frustrating, disappointing, and hurtful if there is no one to listen. All too often, there is not.

Frequently, as a person's death is nearing, his/her ability to interact and respond verbally is diminished, necessitating other forms of communication. The dying person can give us so many cues (e.g., downcast eyes, a furrowed forehead) *if* we are paying attention. In the early days of Isaiah House, a beautiful young woman resident had not verbalized any intelligible words for several days. Clarity seemed no longer possible. Karole was awake and watching us attentively as we cared for her that last Sunday night of her life. At one point, we noticed her facial expression had changed with a slight turn in the corner of her mouth. I said to her, "Karole, your expression is different. Is something troubling you?" And then, to our astonishment, we heard her say clearly and deliberately, "It takes so long." How she needed to express that frustration voiced by countless others since. Would she have told us had we not asked? I think it quite unlikely.

* * *

Turning now to the role of hope, how I appreciate the lovely words of Emily Dickinson:

> "Hope is the thing with feathers
>
> That perches in the soul
>
> And sings the tune — without the words
>
> And never stops at all . . ."[1]

1. Emily Dickinson, "Hope is the thing with feathers," *The Complete Poems of Emily Dickinson,* ed. Thomas H. Johnson (Boston: Little Brown, 1976).

Indeed, hope sustains our spirit. However, it is so very important to realize that hope is ever-changing, evolving from one form to another, even in the worst of times. Some would consider any sort of hope of a dying patient a kind of denial. And, yes, I have heard unrealistic hopes expressed. However, the hopes the dying express are most often deeply rooted in their reality—living day to day, relief of pain, healing troubled relationships, and ultimately a peaceful death. Not a shred of denial here!

When we meet people before welcoming them to Isaiah House, we always ask them a question whose answer will guide us in days ahead: "What are you hoping for now?" A gentle, thoughtful query, it can't be answered with a yes or a no, and the responses have been as varied as the many people themselves. For example, Judy paused before saying, "That's a toughie." We quickly agreed and then waited silently for what seemed a very long time before she answered, "I hope to die peacefully and soon." Judy was just 41 years old.

* * *

A poignant longing to be remembered was an extraordinary lesson we learned from Rose Marie, only 28 years old. At the time of her stay, we were also caring for Anna, just ten years older. Anna's life had been chaotic and complicated. In contrast, Rose Marie seemed demure, almost child-like. Both women were mothers and, sadly, had many regrets. One Saturday we went to Rose Marie's room to tell her we believed Anna would die soon. She did, in fact, within that very hour. Though these two women had never met, they were very much aware of each other's presence in the house, now their home. I asked Rose Marie if she might want to send any comforting parting thoughts to Anna. However, surprisingly, she posed some very practical questions. Was Anna awake, talking, in pain, afraid?—all questions Rose Marie might undoubtedly have had about her own impending death. She then paused, and with a far greater intensity than I ever could have imagined, for she was very weak, this young woman asked, "Do you have a memory of Anna?" It occurred to me that she might also be asking, "Will anyone remember me?" I and other caregivers quickly shared with her our memories of Anna—her astonishing strength, pride, resilience, and endurance. Listening intently, Rose Marie seemed relieved to hear this. In her remaining eleven days, we made sure to take her visitors aside. We would tell them of Rose Marie's question and urge them to tell her how they would remember her—how the example of her gentle spirit and courage in the face of the unthinkable would live on in their lives. Such a lesson we learned from this frail girl. Often we tell our residents' families that the funeral is too late. While there is still time, share with your dear ones the thoughts within your hearts. Regrets, chances missed, are so painful.

* * *

Frequently in our caregiving, we encourage the sharing of those feelings, those matters tucked deeply in the heart. Never pressing, we try to create a safe and neutral atmosphere that might facilitate a coming together for residents and their families. Sometimes this happens; other times it simply cannot. Histories are too complicated; hurts are too deep; emotional reserves are too low. Again and again, as caregivers, we open the doors and step back. We cannot enter that hallowed space because it is not ours.

We sometimes must ask families of our residents: Have you told your dear one that it's all right to go when he or she is ready? This is called the permission to die. Not everyone needs to hear this, but many more people do. It is a most sacred permission—so utterly painful to give, so merciful to receive. However, it is important to realize that not just anyone can grant this permission, and we should not be careless in its use. It is from those closest that the dying person needs to hear those releasing words. In our earliest days, Velma lingered far beyond our expectations. "Hasn't anyone told her it's all right to go?" someone asked. Yet, I well knew that it couldn't be just anyone.

Never will I forget a lengthy, very poignant vigil at Isaiah House as we waited for a young man, Pat, to die. Throughout those final hours, his dad stood at the bedside, stroking his son's head and assuring him over and over that he had done so much good in his short life and that it was now okay for him to go. The room was filled with family and friends that night into morning, yet no one but his beloved dad could have given that. Deeply moved, we all felt so privileged to witness this father's profoundly selfless and loving act.

I also remember a time a dear nurse friend of mine was sitting with a young man whose death had seemed imminent for many days. She simply asked him, "Who do you need to tell you it's all right to go?" Without hesitation, he told her. The permission was given, and he was able to die peacefully.

* * *

It is also important to recognize that as death approaches, the body undergoes many significant changes. Rather than challenge and attempt to redirect its failing systems, we should allow that rest as nature mercifully prepares the body to die. Perhaps you already may have witnessed this unfolding of the dying process and observed those changes in a person approaching death. Most obvious are the physical changes, unique to each person. Usually the person no longer wishes to eat or drink as much, and then not at all. He grows weaker each day, feeling a fatigue beyond any ever felt before, and sleeps more and more of the time. These metabolic changes are all normal for this stage. Eventually, with lessening intake, secretions may thicken. As he grows weaker and unable to cough, or swallow, these secretions can collect in the back of the throat, causing a moist or rattling sound. Irregular patterns may change the rate and depth of breathing. Often, it is marked by long periods with no breath (ten to thirty seconds or longer), called apnea. Frequently, as death draws nearer, breathing may become shallower and more rapid. However, for others, respirations change very little. The process simply is what it is. We are each unique in our dying—as we have been in our living.

Also, changes in circulation become apparent as the extremities may feel cool to the touch. The skin color of the arms and hands may change. In Caucasian people, legs and feet may also be bluish or red-blue and blotchy. This is called mottling (when slowing circulation causes the blood to pool beneath the surface of the skin). In people of color, the skin may have a grayish cast. It may be intermittent over many days or continuous in the hours before death. The person may experience loss of bowel or bladder control as both of these functions decrease. Urine color darkens as it becomes more concentrated. In the words of a wise physician I know, the "body is trying to rest." With the exception of hearing, the senses may dim, thus affecting the person's awareness of the world. Occasionally, the dying person may be observed picking at the bedding, as if removing a speck seen only by him. Or, for example, we once cared for a gentleman who would repeatedly extend his right arm, draw it upward, and then back down again. Since Carl had been an operator of heavy machinery, it of course made perfect sense. And Louise, who had been a seamstress, was seen slowly and deliberately sewing an invisible garment with an invisible needle and thread. Such a poignant sight! An understanding of these many changes can greatly ease anxieties regarding their possible occurrence for they are all quite normal.

* * *

Less visible but perhaps of greater importance are the changes within one's spirit. In the words of Stanislavsky, "the longest and most exciting journey is the journey inward."[2] We should regard such changes with attentive reverence since they often reveal where the person is on her journey. Many years ago we were fortunate to have among our volunteers a young medical student. While talking with a group of his fellow students one afternoon, he wisely reminded them that "We learn all about the physiology of dying, but remember—it's all in the spirit." What a splendid physician he would be.

2. O'Donohue, *Anam Cara,* 127.

I clearly recall an unfortunate incident when, as a relatively new nurse in an acute care hospital, I was approached by a distraught family, seeking some reassurance. Their seriously ill father was sitting upright in bed awake, but he appeared distant from his gathered family. Gazing right through them, not at them, he did not speak. They wondered what they had done to offend him. What was happening? Unfortunately, I did not yet know that it is normal for the dying to lose focus on this world, to disengage from it and withdraw into that inner world of the soul.

An understanding of this reality has allowed us to be thoughtfully sensitive and helpful to our families. With insight into this exquisite spirit journey, many loved ones have been able to appreciate the value of their own quiet, loving, waiting presence at the bedside. This can be a time of extraordinary grace.

Stanislavsky's words are astute. Dying is indeed an *inward* journey we must take. Most likely, we have embarked on other such journeys at various pivotal moments in our lives—in times of discernment and decision, acceptance or rejection. Our very well-being depends upon a willingness to look inward. This insight at our dying time requires the spirit to enter the very heart of its soul. Yet, as our physical energies wane, it becomes difficult, if not impossible, to relate to the outside and the inside at the same time. Nancy Poer, in *Living into Dying*, writes of "layers of personality peeling away like the layers of an onion."[3] That peeling can be exhausting!

3. Nancy Poer, *Living into Dying: A Journal of Spiritual and Practical Death Care for Family and Community* (Philomath, OR: Waldorf Books, 2002), 17.

"I don't like myself today. I'm not feeling very friendly," said Jim one Monday morning. "I don't want any visitors, just my family, quietly." A usually outgoing and friendly man, he was wisely realizing not only his need to go inward but also that he lacked energy to go in both directions. Jim died forty-eight hours later. Conscious until the last hour, he had quietly entered the heart of his soul, preparing for its release. Jim's story beautifully illustrates the withdrawing, the distancing that seems to prepare one for that journey inward and the "soul work" that awaits. Yes, quite simply, there isn't the energy to go in both directions. Often, too, there is disengaging, a pulling away from those things that used to feel important (possessions, places, views of self, etc.) No longer seeming important, they fade into the background. How freeing to one's spirit!

Maria was a beautiful young woman, only in her mid-thirties. On the fireplace mantle in her bedroom, her family placed a large framed photograph of Maria flanked by her two sisters. It was really quite lovely, and everyone exclaimed upon seeing it. Several days before she died, Maria quietly requested that the picture be taken down, and so it was.

* * *

Since our earliest days at Isaiah House, we have called the intensely tender time leading to one's death the "nearing." While in its broadest interpretation, the nearing can last several weeks, we have generally considered it a period of days or hours. It is a hushed and holy time. Always we have sensed a holiness in the house, and it is truly heightened at the time of a resident's "nearing." It is an aura transcending any defined religious or belief system and honoring that of the spirit within each of us. In a way, our resident has turned a corner in his journey, and its end is now in sight. Some have called this nearing time "in the between" as, indeed, the dying person seems to be both here and there. For the Irish, it is called "the thin place." Perhaps it is there that we can catch a glimpse of the other side. It is a time worthy of veneration. With permission, we assist our residents and their families in a variety of ways. These ways are quite possible in any setting in which the dying process is regarded with respect and dignity, and where holistic family-centered care attends the suffering of *all*.

At such times, a candle is offered, symbolizing the sacredness of the time. "This will help to light your way" was the thoughtful comment of a caregiver as she entered a resident's room with a softly glowing candle. And music often fills the air. For many years, we were fortunate to have a dear caregiver who arrived for her shift each week carrying her lovely lyre (a small, harp-like instrument). Her music was a heavenly gift and, on nearing days especially, a summoning of the angels. As we skillfully and gently attend to the physical needs of our dying residents, we are very aware of the intense soul-work going on within their hearts and know that its completion is necessary for the spirit's release.

I've come to believe this may be the hardest work we ever do in this world. Judith, a young mother of two children, cried out just two hours before her death, "I feel as if I am in labor." Dying is indeed a laboring—to release one's spirit. The peaceful face of one who has completed this hard work is ethereal in its beauty and luminosity as it radiates acceptance, serenity, a peace within—a gift beyond measure for both the dying person and those who love her.

Waiting for birth and waiting for death are parallel in intensely personal and powerful ways. Those who care for the dying have aptly been called their midwives. It is my favorite image of this holy work, wherever it may occur.

> *"It was so peaceful; it was so natural . . .*
> *It was so peaceful; it was so natural."*
>
> —Describing her dear one's death,
> Mary repeated this phrase over and over again.

3

Being with the Dying

The Lessons Continue

"We are closest to God in our compassionate moments."

SADLY, ONE of his closest, dearest friends never came to visit my father in his final days. How terribly disappointing, for Dad missed the opportunity to say goodbye, which he very much wanted and needed to do. It was truly a great loss for both of these two good friends. Why, when living those last days must a person feel like an alien being, someone less than he always was? So often this happens. What might be the reasons?

"I'm afraid I won't know what to say." Not surprisingly, this was a frequent response to a question on our Isaiah House volunteer application that asked what apprehensions the person might have about being with the dying. How sad that this has kept many from visiting a seriously ill friend or family member since, in reality, our loving presence and listening heart are far more important than any words we might say.

This is true in part because the world of the dying person is changing. She lies in bed waiting, abilities and bodily integrity slipping away, no longer feeling useful, productive or needed—the values our society so reveres. The person is in a very real sense simply being. And it is into this state of simply being that the dying person invites us. Know, though, that the dying have an uncanny ability to see through us, to know if we are comfortable in their presence. They can size us up pretty quickly. Here there is no room for deception of any sort—for dying is too pure a time for that. So we must be authentically present as they are to us.

Sometimes this means simply sitting in silence. Laden with sensory overload, our society fares poorly with silence. It makes us so uncomfortable. But Elisabeth Kubler-Ross has rightly spoken of the silence that goes beyond words. It is truly golden and often all that is needed.

At other times, being present means simply listening. Great emphasis today is placed upon what we say and how we say it. Many courses teach us how to be effective speakers. Seldom do we see a course on enhancing our listening skills. Expediency rules as answering machines, faxes, emails, and tweets flood our lives with abbreviated shortcuts to communication, and our ability to listen when we are so often in a hurry must struggle to survive. But it is important to listen to the dying. And we must listen in ways we have never listened before, with eyes, ears, hands, and hearts.

For what, though, should we listen? A wise teacher once told his audience of caregivers, "Sit and do nothing. Just listen to the stories." As I will discuss in more detail later, telling our stories at life's ending plays a unique role in the process of letting go. Its importance should not be minimized. The Quakers have a lovely saying—"To listen a soul into disclosure and discovery is the greatest service one human being can do for another."[1] We must preserve listening as the oldest and most powerful tool of healing. It is in real danger of becoming extinct. Remember, too, that often the dying ask questions for which they expect no answers. They simply need to express fears, perceptions of their condition and, yes, their longings too. A devoted grandmother living her final days might wonder what she will wear to her beloved granddaughter's wedding a full year ahead. She may very well know, somewhere deep within, that she will not see that long anticipated family event. Yet, how lovely to imagine it—and to say it aloud. What a gift one gives who listens without judgment but with heart.

It is also always appropriate to be compassionate. As has been said, we are closest to God in our compassionate moments. But what does it really mean to be compassionate? In a book entitled *Compassion*, Henri Nouwen writes, "Compassion asks us to go where it hurts, to enter into places of pain, to share in the brokenness, fear, confusion, and anguish. Compassion challenges us to cry out with those in misery, to mourn with those who are lonely, to weep with those in tears. Compassion requires us to be weak with the weak and powerless with the powerless. Compassion means full immersion in the condition of being human."[2] Are we willing to take such a risk? That we are will be evident to the dying and of immeasurable value to their dying process.

1. Douglas V Steere, *Gleanings: A Random Harvest* (Nashville: Upper Room, 1986).

2. Henry Nouwen, Donald P. McNeill, and Douglas A. Morrison, Compassion: *A Reflection on the Christian Life* (New York: Image Books Doubleday, 1982), 4.

Reminiscence, too, is always of great value. "What should we talk about? It seems trifling to talk about the weather, given what's happening." It was just three days before Tim's death, and his sister was visiting from Florida. Though his responsiveness was waning, Tim was still very much aware of his surroundings. At our suggestion, his sister closed the door and sat very close to the head of her brother's bed, so she could add her touch to their connection and allow their sharing to be intimate as family talks often are. An hour later, she emerged from the room tearful, yet smiling and radiant. It had been so wonderful! Tim had added to his sister's reminiscence with an occasional tear, comment, or chuckle. He had truly participated in the review she had facilitated. Reminiscence is such a tender vehicle for healing. And healing went in both directions that day.

This is a good lesson for each of us to remember for our own lives. If you should find yourself engaging in life review, or participating in that of a dear one, don't be afraid to recall those events tender to your heart, those that may have been disappointing, hurtful, or painful. They have all been woven into the fabric of that life. And very likely it will be our sorrows, our losses, and disappointments that have most strengthened our character, making us who we are. Remember them—and let them go.

Several years later, as another young man lay dying, I was listening in a nearby room as his parents lamented their beloved son's loss of a future and all that it may have held for him—and for them. Their hearts were breaking. When a pause permitted a change in direction, I gently asked, "Tell me, what was Peter like when he was a little boy?" With a soft, sad smile, his mother described this most sensitive and thoughtful of her children. "He taught me more about unconditional love, acceptance, and forgiveness than anyone else," she said. These were no small accomplishments for one so young. I encouraged Peter's parents to hold fast to this beautiful legacy their son would leave and to thank him for it *while there was time.*

I also fondly remember a kindly man I befriended during my hospital nursing days who was suffering from cancer and had frequent admissions for chemotherapy. Given the rapid pace of an acute care setting, there was little time or opportunity to just "be" with any patient. One afternoon when my shift had ended and my charting was finally done, I returned to my patient's room where I found him sitting alone. Closing his door a bit, I joined him for a visit. I don't believe I even knew about life review then, yet somehow, that's what happened. I asked if he might tell me how he had met his wife, whom I had met, and with a smile he began.

All lives are a blending of joys and sorrows, and his was no exception. Gradually, the story unfolded—the sweet glow of the earliest years, living in the country, the blessing of children and their growing, a tragic farming accident claiming the life of a beloved son, and on and on. Lengthy pauses interrupted the story telling — pauses during which I said nothing, just waited. These quiet pauses are necessary to allow time for the gathering of more thoughts as well as to signal permission to continue on. As my patient ended his story, he smiled softly and said, "I haven't thought of these events in so many years—this feels so good." I have never forgotten this dear man's telling of his story. I've wondered if perhaps his reminiscing may have surfaced some issues that needed completion or closure while time remained for such "finishings"—a gift along his journey's way.

Here we find yet another lesson for us all. Because the texture of our lives is generally uneven, so too will be our life review. It needs to be. We can't separate ourselves from our stories. They are who we are. And if review at life's ending can be so validating and affirming, it can be also at other times. We needn't wait until we're dying. We simply need someone to listen.

* * *

While it is important to listen to the dying, it is also important for them to hear us. It was near 8:00 that Saturday morning as we quietly gathered at her bedside. Lois, whom we had welcomed just days earlier, seemed moments from her death, a bit sooner than we might have anticipated. Since her children were out of town, we were alone in our vigil. Just then her phone rang. Gently, I explained to her daughter that her beloved mother was dying. I then placed the phone to Lois's ear while encouraging her daughter to speak from her heart because her mom could still hear. As Lois was drawing her final breaths, her expression softened sweetly in response to the loving words. I was able to share this remarkable sight with this anguished daughter. It was a precious gift for both women.

Frequently we have placed the phone to the ear of a resident who is no longer verbally responsive, thus allowing the person to hear the words of someone special. And again and again, we have observed a telling response, either in the person's expression or an attempt to speak. One young man living a great distance away had such a "visit" with a beloved uncle and we, of course, described his uncle's response to him. Later that same day, the nephew phoned to ask if we might again place the phone to his uncle's ear because he had further thoughts he wished to express. The need to hear—and to be heard—is significant for all of us.

So many of our efforts at Isaiah House are directed at minimizing regrets that our residents and/or their dear ones may be harboring. Oh! They are so painful! So often, things waiting to be said, waiting to be heard, are put on hold until the *right time*. Yet, there is no assurance that right time will ever come. All too common instances of sudden and tragic deaths are stark reminders of this regrettable reality. No time for the thank you's, for forgiveness (in both directions), for expressions of affection and, ultimately, for goodbyes. At the bedside of those who are dying, we are reminded of the wisdom of not procrastinating, of following our heart's nudges, of living fully in each precious moment.

I remember a woman who had come to see her dying friend. I asked her how the visit was going. "It's so good to be here," she said and then, hesitating slightly, she added, "I wish we could have some time alone. There are some things I'd like to tell her." We then invited the gathered relatives to come to the kitchen for coffee so that she might have some time alone with her beloved friend. Both the person dying and those surrounding should have the opportunity, if they wish, to have time alone—to say those things deepest in the heart—to say goodbye. And the significance of this lesson for all aspects of our lives cannot be overstated. It is important that we always be ready to say those things to those we love.

From the day of her young daughter Mary Kay's arrival at Isaiah House, Catherine had steadfastly expressed her need to be strong. This included her keeping a "stiff upper lip." Days passed and this dear mother, whose heart was surely breaking, continued to "be strong" despite our gentle nudges that she allow herself to be otherwise. And then, one evening Catherine came rushing from her daughter's room to find me. "Oh," she cried, with a beautiful tear-stained smile. "I've crossed a bridge tonight. I was able to cry. We held one another and cried." At last, her mother's tears had given Mary Kay permission to express her feelings. My heart rejoiced in this breakthrough. The aching hearts of these two dear women had been bathed in the healing balm of their tears. They had indeed crossed a bridge.

Another story about crying comes to mind— Joan, a crusty woman in her late 50's, admitted to us that she hadn't always been the nicest person in her life. Yet we found that we enjoyed her presence enormously. One day, a friend who had come to visit was seen to be crying as she left the house. As her caregiver entered the room, Joan said, somewhat pensively, "You know, it's nice to know you're worth someone's tears." Many times I've shared her words with other families and friends who try, so valiantly, to hold back the tears, protecting themselves, protecting others, or so they think. But remember—tears can speak volumes, a tender exchange of these most tender feelings.

Crying has been called the neglected dimension of caring. Being open and authentic means not being afraid to show our tears. Yet so often we try so hard to conceal them, considering them a sign of weakness. They are not! We may be afraid of the emotions these tears could unleash and reveal. But know that your tears can give others the permission to shed their own—a gift in itself. Tears are not only cleansing; they can also offer a release from burdensome fears and anxieties. Ultimately, and mercifully, tears can be healing.

* * *

So come once again to the bedside of a dying person, this time with lessons in hand. Don't be afraid. Remember, you needn't say anything—*just be*. If you sense the need to speak, let it come from your heart. If any of your "inside tears" seem to be coming to the surface, let them. They will speak for you. Touch is a beautiful connection for which many people long. You will know if your dear one is comfortable with this or not. A hand placed lightly on the person's forearm is a gentle link and may enhance the closeness you desire.

If there are hurts that weigh heavily, acknowledge them to yourself and your dear one. Then let them go and move on. This is not a time to hold on to old baggage. It is too heavy to be carried any longer, and it's getting in the way. Be blessed by that merciful release that flows from forgiveness. This may be your last visit. Don't waste those precious moments and risk having painful regrets. Be assured that peaceful closure will be a source of healing for you both. And for you, it will bring great comfort as you carry its poignant memory for the rest of your days.

Surely, our lives would be sadly diminished without our lessons from the dying. In our earliest days at Isaiah

House, a lovely young woman expressed a slight unease while preparing to be a volunteer caregiver. She was, however, determined to try. Several weeks later, I cautiously inquired how was it going for her. Her response was immediate and enthusiastic. "Oh. I love it! The rest of my life needs me to be here each week. It's helping me to keep things in perspective." Some of the caregivers have suggested that being in the house is somewhat like a retreat time, and they have relished its peaceful calm. Still others, mindful of our ability to maintain the comfort and dignity of both our residents and their families, have proclaimed they no longer fear death nor the getting there. These are no small perks! And they are there for all of us who care for the dying, who are not afraid to be with the dying.

> *"Of all sad words of tongue and pen, the saddest are these,*
> *'It might have been.'"*

—John Greenleaf Whittier

4

The Gentle Gifts of Caring

The Hospice Way

"Our lives have been transformed by this."

IT WASN'T until his funeral that Pat's surprising words were revealed. "I didn't realize it was so easy to die." We had not heard those words before, and clearly they deserved some reflection. I've long believed with all my heart that it is quite possible to live fully while dying for I have witnessed this many times. And how beautifully Pat had done just that. "My brother is having the time of his life," announced his sister shortly after his arrival at Isaiah House. Pat's enthusiastic spirit charmed us all as he shared many wonderful stories, even while inviting the stories of others. It has been said that stories are maps telling us where to go. Perhaps Pat was finding his way. His days were rich and filled with meaning even as his illness progressed, and his body grew weaker. In the midst of the daily changes, his personhood seemed to remain intact. With equanimity, Pat one day declared, "I am declining, you know." And several days later, "I think this is it." Soon after, it was.

"I didn't realize it was so easy to die." In case you may consider that an oversimplification, let me try to explain.

Dying actually *is* hard work as one strives to attain integration and wholeness in the face of disintegration, loss of control, loss of body image, loss of who we were. The workings of spirit, in the midst of all the bodily ßchanges, are often the most daunting. At the same time, these efforts can be most rewarding, leading to fulfillment and meaning beyond one's expectations. Healing of one's heart and relationships frequently requires complicated, painful, even exhausting efforts—both for the dying person and his dear ones. Mercifully, the transforming blessings of these efforts can allow a peaceful closure *for all*.

The dying person can truly engage in his dying process when he is surrounded by compassionate caregivers to accompany him on this final journey—when painful or distressing symptoms are relieved—when he knows that his loved ones are being supported. And yes, dying can then be perceived as "easy." We will always be grateful not only for Pat's bright light, but for the many lights that have guided us through the years, including the gentle light of the *hospice philosophy*.

* * *

For many of you, hospice may be a familiar term. For others, its meaning may be less clear. More than a place, hospice is essentially a philosophy, an attitude, a manner of caring. It was in the 1960's that renowned Swiss psychiatrist Elisabeth Kubler-Ross opened the windows and let in the fresh air of our understanding and appreciation for the extraordinary dynamics of dying. This brave pioneer ventured to the bedsides of countless dying individuals and listened, listened, listened. She began to explore the depths of this profound and intimate passage that awaits each of us. Her wise, insightful, and illuminating writings over several decades led the way for others to join in thoughtful discernment of this topic that had for so long been avoided by the multitudes. We all owe Kubler-Ross an enormous debt of gratitude for opening those windows to a more compassionate view of death and dying.

Another wonderful pioneer, Dame Cecily Saunders, founded the modern hospice movement with the establishment of St. Christopher's Hospice in London in 1967. She will long be lovingly remembered for her beautiful words. "You matter because you are you. You matter to the last moment of your life and we will do all that we can, not only to help you die peacefully, but also, to live until you die."[1] One of my favorite stories tells of a gentleman visiting St. Christopher's for a tour. As Dr. Saunders took him from room to room, her incredulous visitor exclaimed, "My good woman, you have no intensive care unit." Her immediate reply was, "My good man, every unit is an intensive care unit." And indeed, holistic care is just that—intensive care of the whole person—physical, spiritual emotional, and social. We are challenged to view more than a set of physical symptoms but also the uniqueness of the person's spirit.

In its earliest days, the voice of hospice seemed restrained. Because the hospice approach to embracing the dying process was introduced in a climate of death denial, it took some time to gain a foothold into our collective ways of thinking about dying. Thankfully, this voice has become more persistent and passionate as it offers a sensible,

1. Cicely Saunders, "Care of the Dying: The Problem of Euthanasia," Nursing Times 72 (1976): 1004.

practical, and more compassionate approach to caring for the dying and their families. Responding to the many poignant concerns and anxieties surrounding terminal illness, this gentle philosophy allows death to come in its own time and in its own way. Let's explore in greater detail what this means.

* * *

A frequent question asked by caregivers of the dying over the years has been, "Aren't most people afraid to die?" Here, one's traditions, spirituality, and religious beliefs can come into play. Is death viewed as an ending or beginning, or both? Certainly, it is a venture into the unknown. We've never done it before. However, it doesn't seem to be so much the moment of death that is feared as it is the process of "getting there." Will I be in pain, suffering; will I be alone? Feelings of helplessness, hopelessness, and loss of control run rampant, often extending to those surrounding the dying person too. It can be a terrifying time.

In the most caring way, the hospice philosophy addresses and eases those fears and provides a way for caregivers to accompany and support the dying person and her dear ones for the time remaining. As David Gregory and John English so eloquently state in the *Journal of Palliative Care*, "Compassionate care is possible only by being present and engaging with those who suffer. This necessitates an act of commitment on the part of the caregiver. Presence transcends the self and represents an invitation to share the journey and come alongside and be allowed to see, to share, to touch, and to hear this brokenness, vulnerability, and suffering of another. Only through the mingling of personhoods can genuine compassion unfold—*sufferers lead and caregivers follow rather than being in control.*"[2] This last phrase summarizes well the essence, the heart of hospice caregiving.

Caregivers-to-be are also likely wondering what they might expect to encounter as they begin this journey. Perhaps this is the first time they've been with a dying person. It's helpful, then, for them to know that repeated losses are a hallmark of the dying process, as the dying person struggles to retain her authenticity and the integrity of her personhood. It is no small task because a vital part of our human condition is our need to be in control. How very important our choices are to us, defining who we are, who we will become, and how we will be remembered. Sometimes we choose wisely, sometimes foolishly. Yet, our ability to maintain some degree of control usually remains intact. We often speak of one's agenda, as in "Whose agenda is this— yours or mine?" We really want it to be our own—more of that control. Journeying with the dying casts a very different light on issues of control, on whose agenda this is. For hospice caregivers, our own preferences for care must often take a back seat as we strive to honor the wishes of our dying residents, even if they are counter to ours.

Don, a quiet, studious man, dealt with his need to remain in control with a bit of wry humor. One afternoon, noting that his bed linens were quite rumpled, I asked if I might straighten his sheets. "No, you may not," he responded with a slight smile. After a moment, I said with amusement, "Don would you say that your need to not have me

2. David Gregory and John English, "The Myth of Control: Suffering in Palliative Care," *Journal of Palliative Care* 10 (1994): 18.

straighten the sheets is greater than my need to do it?" And then, again with a smile, "Yes, I'd say that was true." About thirty minutes later, I approached Don and expressed my very real concern that the wrinkles in the sheets threatened his quite fragile skin. He then allowed me to proceed. However, it had been important to respect his initial resistance, to allow him at least a modicum of control.

Suzanne, a young woman valiantly struggling to maintain control, asked one day, "Would you please move my overbed table two inches to the left?" So often since, I have reflected upon her request and the physical limitations of her world—that world bound by four walls. For Suzanne, no more planning for tonight's dinner . . . or next summer's vacation. So for her to retain any control was very important.

Still another young woman, also named Mary Kay, plaintively declared on the evening of her welcoming to Isaiah House, "I've had to let go of so many things." She had to relinquish so many aspects of mothering her five children. A college degree she attained later in life had led to a job she loved and now had to leave behind. Surgery and treatments had taken their toll, and now the progression of her illness rendered her bedfast and partially paralyzed. She had indeed "let go of so many things." Therefore, it was vital that she be allowed control and choices, that her independence and dignity be maintained as long as possible. And, of course, it was.

So we see that a basic tenet of the hospice philosophy is that of patient control. We who practice hospice caregiving must always remain sensitive to the pattern of loss that accompanies the dying process—the loss of independence, mobility, a body part, one's hair, privacy, dignity. Imagining the impact of these and other losses can help us to empathize more fully and better understand the frustrations that often attend them. It is so considerate to honor those choices that are within the bounds of safety and reality. Melvin was a young man whose head and neck cancer had greatly impaired his ability to eat. One day he surprised us by announcing he would like to go to a legendary eating place in town famous for its garbage plate special. Well, why not, we thought. Early that snowy December evening, his volunteer caregiver very carefully escorted this frail young man to the car and to the restaurant. Melvin ordered the garbage plate, pouring upon it every condiment on the table. He was able to enjoy but a taste, yet we well know his satisfaction went far beyond that. Choices—control—remained with him. For his caregivers, the satisfaction in honoring his wish to live in the moment in this way was a blessing in itself. So it is important for the dying person to know his control will be encouraged and maintained as long as possible. It isn't hard to care for the dying if we let them tell us how they wish their last days to be.

* * *

The stresses of care giving can be many and overwhelming. It is for this reason that the hospice philosophy views the patient and family as a unit of care for anxiety and concern are truly felt in both directions. How could the suffering of a dying person not resonate with those who love her? Is that not the nature of love: we feel with and for one another? Sometimes the person who is most hurting and in need of care isn't the patient but a family member or friend.

The hospice philosophy also helps put the concept of hope in perspective. Fearful of taking away hope, many physicians may give an unrealistic prognosis to a terminally ill patient, suggesting that she has a length of time remaining that is highly unlikely. Not only can this lead to false hopefulness but, more importantly, it could interfere with a patient's preparation for death—both her right and her need. Some family members, too, in misguided efforts to protect, often color or hide the truth about their loved one's condition. So often this is a reflection of their own inability to accept the painful reality they are facing—that their loved one is going to die. After so many years of being with and learning from the dying, I believe the fear of taking away hope is unfounded. Once we are beyond experiencing the devastating initial impact of sad news, we can better grapple with its truth than with its distortions. The hope evolving through one's illness is remarkably resilient. One's ability to adapt, however, is sustained by truthfulness every step of the way, beginning with the diagnosis.

A woman whose family did not want her to know she was dying was referred to Isaiah House. Heavens! Without this awareness, how could she possibly engage in her dying process? Such an indignity. We could not be part of this deception so sadly she could not be accepted as a resident. Historically, this kind of truth distortion was viewed as protective. It was feared that knowing the gravity of an illness would take away hope. There seemed to be little understanding that, rather than being taken away, hope—ever changing—would maintain the spirit until death. Perhaps if there had been a recognition of the subtleties of the dying process and its ability to transform lives, it would have not seemed necessary to protect people from its sting.

At other times it is the caregiver who cannot give up an unrealistic hope. Judy's serenity had inspired us as she calmly prepared for her death. Her beloved aunt, however, was still praying for a miracle even as, with aching heart, she watched the steady decline of her precious niece. With gentle patience, accepting Aunt Marion where she was, we continued to quietly support her hopefulness. We were confident it was evolving toward a different awareness, for this is the nature of hope within illness. It wasn't until Judy herself implored, "Don't do this to me" (pray for a miracle) that Aunt Marion tearfully replied, "All right, Judy. I'll pray for whatever it is you are praying for." Such a moment of reckoning for these two dear women. Judy died peacefully the following day.

Hospice caregiving offers a poignant opportunity to minimize painful regrets (about which I have written earlier). Many intimate moments will invite a sharing of hearts. Remember, this "gift time" is precious and so very tenuous. Don't let it slip by unfulfilled. Imagine that you have discovered, upon visiting, that your dear friend is alone, as if waiting for you. You may never again have this chance. Embrace this moment fully and share what is in your heart. What a gift for you both! It has become apparent to me that most people in a waiting mode, such as those witnessing the decline of a loved one, seem to feel there will be more time. Even when they learn of a prognosis that indicates the person has little time left, they may still believe—or want to believe— there will be more of it. But do remember, our lives are very fragile, especially when we are very ill. Conditions can change in a proverbial heartbeat. There may never again be this opportunity to draw to a close this loving relationship that is so dear to you. Please don't delay, waiting for a time that may never come.

* * *

The healing of spirit in hospice philosophy has been described as an interior healing, the health of the soul, the healing of relationships. It is a broad definition of healing. For spiritual as well as other forms of caregiving, it is important that we take cues from our patient. That requires skillful listening and an attitude of acceptance. *A compassionate presence itself can provide spiritual support.* A resident at Isaiah House once stated that such support emerges from sustained bonds with a caring person. The same resident went on to say, "If you give spiritual support to someone, you are giving everything you have. It's never turning away from that person. It's always being there for that person in good times and in bad times. If you offer spiritual support, it is being there with God's love extending to them through you." How precious is this spirit, always to be regarded with reverence and, often, with amazement for its resiliency, its ability to spring back after repeated hurts, is quite astonishing!

The hospice approach to death also focuses on palliative care. The essence of such care is to offer relief without attempting to cure. A key goal, rather, is to allow the dying person to remain as comfortable and interactive as possible so that he can engage in his dying process. Or stated differently, living while dying is a key tenet of the hospice philosophy, with the emphasis being on living.

It is first important to note that for this to happen, a dying person's pain and other distressing symptoms must be addressed—and they can be. Know that they can be!! Anxiety, restlessness, shortness of breath, nausea, vomiting, and constipation are among a constellation of distressing symptoms other than, though often related to, pain. We have a variety of antidotes for each of these discomforts. If we hope to enhance the quality of the life remaining, *each* symptom deserves prompt attention. Also, keep in mind that the anticipation of pain can be very frightening. Fortunately, much has been learned over the years about skillful symptom management as we've come to better understand various origins of pain and the pharmaceutical agents to which each will respond. Always, the goal is to achieve the optimal level of comfort with the optimal level of alertness. It really is possible to do this well. When troubling symptoms are treated, the dying person can better live fully in the moment as death nears.

A certain resident who was able to live fully as she was dying comes to mind. Mary left a message on our answering machine. "I have terminal lung cancer. I'd like to come to live at Isaiah House." Living alone, Mary no longer had any family. Though many friends cherished her, they were unable to assume her care. We were grateful to welcome this extraordinary human being, and we grew to love her dearly. While exclaiming that "my bags are packed, and I'm ready to go," Mary continued to be immersed in her living. She waited eagerly for our garden's first crocus, then tulip, then iris, and she saw them all. Mary avidly continued watching the television news and became appalled when a Washington check scandal surfaced one Sunday morning.

She urgently requested and signed her absentee ballot for an April primary. Despite her nausea, she dreamed of and requested a variety of savory treats, knowing they might not stay down too long. She remained interested in the lives of her friends and caregivers.

Mary personified living fully in the moment and did not waste a single one. While proclaiming she was "ready to go," she seemed quite delighted to still be here, to remain the vibrant, remarkable woman she had always been. She truly did *live* at Isaiah House. Indeed, Mary was in our "school" a professor *par excellence*, and she was blessed with a gentle death. Many such illuminating insights gained over the years in our school have guided us to new understandings of long-held perceptions.

One such perception is the often-voiced concern of a dying person about being a burden. Yet, might this phrase be expressing fears deeper than that of being a burden, fears perhaps more related to giving up independence, control, privacy, even dignity; fear of being alone, of not being heard, of no longer being valued as the person you have always been, of losing hope? Linda, a 46-year-old mother of six children who had been taking turns caring for her, said with great sadness, "It would be far easier for me to care for one of my children who was dying than to have them care for me." What a painful reversal of roles.

In a hospice setting, whatever its nature, the fear of being burdensome is often relieved when the dying person comes to appreciate that in allowing others to care, to create a caring community, an opening is created, an opportunity for others to give back, to show how deeply they care, how deeply they love. It also offers a chance for caregivers to be

relieved of the haunting feelings of helplessness upon seeing the inevitable decline in their dear one's condition. In a
variety of settings, I've been privileged to witness the im-
mense satisfaction and comfort felt by family and friends as
they ministered to the needs of their dear ones. Indeed, I've
known this myself, and its gift is priceless.

I will never forget a remarkable and delightful young
woman whose gentle humor and beautiful smile warmed
the hearts of all who met her. How very fortunate we were
to welcome Cathy Ann to Isaiah House. Since several com-
ponents of her care were quite arduous, her devoted family members offered to participate. They were grateful to
show this precious woman how much they loved her. On
a number of occasions, friends who came by to visit were
also invited to join in the caregiving, and they did so eagerly
and with great tenderness. They so wanted to help! With
gracious humility, Cathy Ann allowed us all to cradle her in
our loving care. Everyone was blessed in those moments. In
hospice, those moments are everywhere.

Not only does hospice allow loved ones to be involved
in the care of the dying person if he wishes, it also offers a
place for what has been called the consecration of death.
Again, this place may be in any setting that reverently
honors this peaceful passage from one life to the next—a
caring that, while focusing on the dying person, extends to
those who watch and wait, suffer and quietly withdraw. It
becomes a hallowed time for those who choose this direction of care and a mercifully natural death.

For many of those contemplating a caregiver role,
the prospect may seem daunting. Without compassionate
guidance and support, it surely is. So many families have

thankfully found the entire situation changed by the intervening of hospice. "Our whole family has been enveloped," exclaimed a grateful family member. Reflecting upon that very basic hospice mandate that the patient and family are a unit of care, they are indeed enveloped by the understanding concern and care of the hospice team. Families are assured they are not alone in an overwhelming circumstance. No longer feeling isolated and desperate, they can focus on relationships, on matters of the heart, savoring and cherishing the precious time remaining. This truly can be a time like no other and, yes, it can be transforming.

The many families transformed by the hospice experience bear witness to the wisdom of choosing this compassionate alternative. Whether it be a dedicated bed in a hospital or nursing home, a freestanding hospice facility, or the sanctity of one's home, the support of hospice eases this transition for all. But do remember—this choice of hospice should never be made in a crisis moment or as a last resort. As with the other important decisions in our lives, a choice for hospice deserves our careful, enlightened consideration. All of this comes back to the great need for us to have these extremely important and vital end-of-life conversations sooner—now. Please don't wait!

Your awareness of available options in times of life-threatening illness needs to include palliative care, now a certified and highly respected medical and nursing specialty. These compassionate practitioners, joined by other similarly prepared professional caregivers, have formed consultation groups in many hospitals across the country. With the goal of enhancing the quality of the life remaining, however long that may be, these most caring team members offer sensitive guidance and support to patients and families living with a terminal illness. Issues such as pain, nausea, anxiety, and fatigue, among others, can be skillfully managed and relieved. This allows a fullness of life not otherwise possible. Emotional support and counsel, consistent with the holistic nature of care, is a vital dimension of concern. Such helpful consultations not only really do make a difference—they also lay the foundation for those last days or weeks, hopefully in hospice. One ideally leads to the other!

As with the choice for hospice, a physician's referral can set the wheels toward palliative care in motion. For many families, this choice has proven to be a merciful intervention. Isn't this what we would hope for ourselves or our dear ones? Know that this journey need not be as overwhelming as you may have anticipated.

"Suffering in others is relieved in so much as we are prepared to enter into it ourselves."

—Leonard Cheshire

5

Coming to Life Again

Finding Your Way through Bereavement

"I don't know how to do it."

So FAR my reflections have dealt with issues surrounding an anticipated death and, thus, anticipatory grieving—the mourning we do when faced with the imminent death of someone we love. Mercifully, this experience can offer the dying person and her family members some preparation time and an opportunity to minimize regrets and complete the unfinished business that can bring about peaceful closure for *all*. Still, as night follows the day, so too does a period of bereavement follow death. And it must be acknowledged that even with an awareness of impending loss, death's moment of arrival can be staggering.

Unfortunately, society has often sadly misunderstood grieving, dealing with it poorly, if at all. We hardly know how to begin this difficult work that is unique to each of us. Deeply devoted to his wife, Tom had been a most loving and attentive caregiver throughout her many years of illness. We welcomed Bernice to Isaiah House for her last two weeks. Soon after her death, Tom came by to visit, as family members so often do. Plaintively, he shared—"I went to the library to find some books about bereavement. I don't know how to do it." In reality, his grieving had begun— even if imperceptively, years earlier as he sadly witnessed his beloved wife's gradual diminishments. He must have mourned each of them. Yet, he felt he had just begun. It was the journey ahead that must have felt so overwhelming. I believe it likely that many others suffering the loss of a dear one are fearful of what is yet to follow and "don't know how to do it." As with the dying process, a further awareness and understanding of bereavement can ease many anxieties.

Sadly, when death comes suddenly, unexpectedly, shattered hearts and lives may have had no time to pre-pare. Death's finality can be devastating, whichever way it occurs. The toll taken by its impact cannot be hastily lessened. Immediate reactions often include shock and disbelief. Gradually and painfully they fade into the over-whelmingly sorrowful reality with which one must live and somehow cope.

It was a frosty November morning, the Monday be-fore Thanksgiving. We were at the cemetery to bury my father. Prayers had been said, and his coffin was lowered into the ground. Family and friends who had gathered quietly began to leave. But I held back, wanting to stay longer, just looking at his coffin in that cold earth. My cousin Bob came over to me and gently said, "It's so hard to leave, isn't it?" He then put his arms around me and held me as I cried. I've never forgotten that moment or Bob, whom I hadn't really known well, but who—at that moment—knew me very well. From his own earlier expe-riences with parental loss, he had sensed my anguish, my need. By simply saying, "It's so hard to leave, isn't it?" he conveyed his compassionate understanding. The barriers were stripped away, and I was able to cry those healing tears—my own grief journey continued.

Grieving takes time—time largely ignored in a society that typically allows three days for funeral arrangements to be completed and then seems to expect all to be back to normal. It simply cannot, nor should it be! Many years ago I came upon a wonderful little article in a bereavement journal entitled "You must get over it." In it, Penny Blaze has written, "You *never* get over it because that would mean you would have to stop loving that person or remembering your life together. This pain we feel is just a reminder that we loved so very deeply. It takes time, commitment, and courage to incorporate such deep pain into ourselves. We have to address the pain directly, feel its power, understand it, and finally befriend it before we can rebuild our lives."[1] With this last sentence, I gratefully recall the words of a dear friend upon her mother's death. "I will take my friend grief by the hand and see where she takes me." A different slant to be sure. My friend well realized that she needed to go through her grief—not over, under, or around it. Here, there are no choices. You must embark upon this very sad journey. Our grieving, despite its painfulness and, yes, it is so painful, is truly essential for our future emotional and physical health.

Experiencing grief has been compared to enduring a stormy sea. In the beginning the grief waves are so high, are packed so close together they almost tip us over. We

1. Penny Blaze, "You Must Get Over It!!!," *Compassionate Friends Brisbane Newsletter* (June/July 2007), accessed March 11, 2011, http://www.uq.net.au/tcfbrisbane/JunJul07.htm#Item%204.

can feel like we might even drown. How do we stay afloat? Yet, mercifully, in time, the sea becomes calmer—and *it will*. But do remember that occasionally, even years later, the waves, some now becoming ripples, will return without warning, catching us unaware. I love this very visual image and am actually grateful for the "ripples" in my own life. Sometimes we even seek them out, those poignant moments of remembering sparked by a fragrance, a sound, a sight. For many years, my youngest sister and I, during an annual visit to the Adirondack Mountains, purposely visited a little pipe and old book store tucked in a busy village. Just opening the door and entering this quaint little shop evoked warm and fragrant memories of our beloved Dad who loved books and so often smoked his pipe. We always stayed and browsed a bit so that our memories could linger a while. Try to believe that the ferocious waves of grief can, in time, become gentler and even comforting. Mercifully, the healing balm of passing time can soften, ease, and make more bearable the ache of your longing for your dear one. That longing will always be there, a tender imprint on your heart.

There is no calendar for grief. I've long appreciated the story of a young man who asked his wise elder, "How long does grief last?" And the answer—"How high is up?" Thomas Moore has written, "Let sadness reveal its timetable rather than subject it to yours. Let life flow through you, making you more and more human."[2] Isn't that beautifully powerful imagery? Letting life flow through you includes

2. Thomas Moore, "Growing through Grief," *Spirituality and Health* (January/February 2007), accessed March 11, 2011, http://www.spiritualityhealth.com/NMagazine/articles.php?id=1646.

allowing yourself to feel *all* the painful emotions that can color the experience of loss. We're not meant to control the feelings that might arise within us. They come from deep inside. Will we become overwhelmed by these emotions or will we feel them and then move on? The choice is ours. But however we may be feeling, know that the healing is happening, almost imperceptively. Our human nature has a natural inclination to recover. And you will have little signs along the way. Be watchful because they will be reassuring.

Kate's young adult son had been killed in a car accident, forever changing the lives of those who loved him. I fondly recall the day she told me with a soft smile, "I whistled today—it was the first time since Connor died." You, too, will have your own stories of re-awakening, feeling again, experiencing moments of joy. In time, those moments will be multiplied in your life, so changed, so different. Ecclesiastes was so very wise in telling us that, for everything, there is a season.

It may be helpful to know that for the grieving heart, repeated telling of the story of the loved one's death helps the person believe what has happened and begin to accept its reality. Talking becomes a therapy of sorts. Sometimes, though, we may be stuck in our grieving. We may need more than the loving listening of our family and friends. At such times, it's possible and so important to seek professional counseling to help move you along on your grief journey. Know that unresolved grief is often linked to depression. Skilled bereavement counselors are well-prepared to deal with the sensitive and often complicated issues that surround grieving. Offering invaluable assistance in a number of ways, hospice bereavement care programs can provide names and contact numbers for counselors in your area. Remember that you don't have to do this alone. There are times when grieving becomes overwhelming, and a person may feel quite lost. A wise and caring professional can help you find your way once again. Such interventions can be truly life-saving. Families are also informed of various support groups, many of which are tailored to the specific loss of a child, spouse, parent, sibling, or friend. This is so very wise because grief support cannot be "one size fits all."

Admittedly, not everyone is comfortable seeking support in a group, so another avenue may work better for them. Yet, for many others, the group setting can be both comforting and enriching as grieving hearts can connect in ways they might not with others. Wonderful stories have been told of lasting friendships formed in those healing times together. Other avenues outside of support groups include hospice mailings that offer supportive information and convey an ongoing remembrance of the loved one who has died and of you who mourn this ongoing sorrow. Thoughtfully planned memorial services, such as Christmas tree lighting ceremonies commemorating those who have died that year, are also offered. These gatherings are especially comforting since survivors often dread their first holidays without their dear one.

While sufferings of spirit, such as guilt, confusion, and anxiety, must be addressed, it is also important not to neglect one's physical health at such a vulnerable time. Sleep disturbances are not at all uncommon. Awakening in the early morning hours or lying awake at night are frequent complaints. Loss of appetite, leading to weight loss, is another. Know that these and other health concerns are common in this sorrow-filled time. Please don't delay in reporting them to your physician. Try to take gentle care of *you* now.

This grief journey does not need to be solitary, nor should it be. However, it is vital to have some quiet time. "We're keeping Mom or Dad busy" is an often heard phrase as families scurry about to keep the grieving person occupied to avoid him/her having too much time to think about the loss. Of course, it's important to be with dear ones at this time, to support and love one another as perhaps you never have before—to grow closer to one another. But we must have time alone, time just "to be"—to feel—to hurt—to cry. And please don't be afraid to cry. Don't avoid what can be a merciful release. Tears have been called the "antifreeze of the soul." Let them flow freely. A little verse by French novelist Leon Bloy long hung on the kitchen wall at Isaiah House, and I have always loved it. "There are places in the heart which do not yet exist and into them suffering enters so that they may have existence." There are lessons in your sorrow. You will never be the same.

Do remember that though you are living a universal human experience, your grief is uniquely yours. No one else knows exactly how you are feeling. Those who have known similar losses may understand a bit, yet not completely, because your sorrow is your own—with its subtleties and nuances known only to you. It may be painful to be reminded of your dear one and yet, don't you always want to be, as you cherish this enduring and precious thread in your life's tapestry that will ever be a part of you?

This lovely Celtic prayer entitled "Walking with Grief" may be helpful:

Do not hurry
as you walk with grief.
It does not help the journey.

walk slowly,
pausing often:
do not hurry
as you walk with grief.

Be not disturbed
by memories that come unbidden.
Swiftly forgive:
and let God speak for you
unspoken words.
Unfinished conversation
will be resolved in Him.
Be not disturbed.

Be gentle with the one
who walks with grief.
If it is you,
Be gentle with yourself.
Swiftly forgive:
walk slowly,
pausing often.

Take time, be gentle
As you walk with grief.[3]

* * *

Over many years, I've come to believe there are gifts within
our grieving—life changing gifts. It is quite possible to

3. The Northumbria Community, "Walking With Grief," in *Celtic
Daily Prayers and Readings from the Northumbria Community* (New
York: HarperOne, 2002), 255.

emerge from your sorrow with greater compassion, under-standing, and a heightened capacity to love more fully and more deeply. A greater compassion—how desperately our hurting world longs for such gentle gifts of caring for the sufferings of others. Perhaps you have found yourself be-ing touched by others facing a loss similar to yours. I know that even more than forty years after my children died, I find myself moved upon reading the obituary notice of a child and silently send a prayer in the family's direction. How could we help but resonate with what we have known? With your own wounded heart, you are able to listen with what has been called the "ear of your heart." Still cradling the image of your own dear one, you are much more finely tuned to the pathos of another. What could be more beauti-ful—our own humanity touching the humanity of another, hearts touching hearts—no small accomplishment. It is a poignant testimonial to your dear one's memory.

Perhaps you may find yourself walking with someone who is grieving. This will be a tender task. In her lovely little book, *Seasons of Your Heart*, Macrina Weiderkehr writes so movingly about her own impressions of the Beatitudes that she seems to be talking to you. "Blessed are you if you are so full of compassion you see the need before it is spoken. Blessed are you if you can offer to others a heart that feels their sorrow, a heart that can wait quietly beside them, and a heart that doesn't try to hurry the healing."[4] Oh, yes! I urge you also not to tiptoe around or refrain from saying the name of the person who has died. That name, ever trea-sured, is but a breath away. So often, barely into the con-

4. Macrina Wiederkehr, *Seasons of Your Heart: Prayers and Reflection* (San Francisco: HarperOne, 1991), 378.

versation with a grieving person, I have learned to ask the name of the person who has died. That awareness allows me to more sensitively make reference to him/her throughout our conversation. It's a way of indicating that the dear one is very real; yes, this event really has happened; and yes, her memory is cherished.

Throughout our lives joys and sorrow seem to be intermingled, one coloring the intensity of the other. Kahil Gibran once wrote, "The deeper that sorrow carves within your heart, the more joy it can contain." And isn't our joy more wondrous given the depth of our sorrow? How could we really know one without the other? These contrasts seem quite necessary for a fullness of life and living. Remember, we have but the moment we're in. So clearly now, because of our grieving, we can appreciate this wisdom and live differently because of it. Surely, this is no small gift—and one to hold fast. It might even be considered one of life's blessings in disguise.

"To mourn is to be given a second heart."[5]

—Macrina Weiderkehr

5. Wiederkehr, *Seasons of Your Heart*, 98.

6

Preparing for Your Own Death

The Choices Are Yours

"We know not the hour nor the day."

THE GENTLE heart of Geshe Kelsang Gyatso, internationally renowned teacher of Buddhism and Meditation Master, has guided us well . . . "Preparing for death is one of the kindest and wisest things we can do for both ourselves and others."[1] But how do we begin such a daunting task, one which we would rather prefer to ignore—this reminder that we will die. However sobering, it is essential that we acknowledge our mortality . . . our lives will not go on forever.

It has been said that dying is a developmental stage, as have been each of the preceding others. And haven't the other stages asked of us a certain preparation? High school and college students, after considering various career paths, study diligently in pursuit of their choices; young parents anticipating the new baby's arrival eagerly prepare the nursery and themselves; those in the workforce strive to prepare wisely for retirement years. Would it not then seem a natu-

1. Geshe Kelsang Gyatso, *Living Meaningfully, Dying Joyfully* (Glen Spey, NY: Tharpa Publications, 1999).

ral expectation that we put things in order—in preparation for our death? In his early 60's, my Dad pensively declared one day, "You begin to wonder what it is that will take you." Is this not a question that is familiar to many of us? And then, *how will it be?*, and a bit further—and *how do I want it to be?*

As noted earlier, we know neither the hour nor the day of our death. For some, yes, it will come suddenly, without warning. Yet, for many more, it will be anticipated. However it may be, remember that your choices, if documented, will decide your manner of care if or when you are determined to be in an irreversible medical condition and are unable to make your own decisions any longer. This circumstance could result from a sudden event such as a heart attack, a stroke, an accident—or a lingering illness for which curative measures are no longer appropriate. There are countless situations for which the sad term "irreversible" might apply. Others could include end-stage heart, lung, or kidney disease and multiple organ failure resulting from a massive infection or a variety of other causes. Unfortunately, they are not age-specific.

Little did three young American women realize they would sadly become famous in their dying, their stories legendary over the past four decades. In 1975, Karen Ann Quinlan (no relation to me), consumed alcohol and valium at a party, collapsed, and became unconscious. Twice she stopped breathing for fifteen minutes or more, thus suffering brain damage and lapsing into a coma. She was kept alive on a ventilator. After several months, it was apparent that there was no improvement in her condition. In a much-publicized legal battle, her parents requested that her life-prolonging care be discontinued. Although the ventilator wasn't removed until the following year, Karen Ann's tube feedings continued, so their beautiful daughter remained alive for almost a decade. She died from pneumonia in a New Jersey nursing home in 1985. She was just 35 years old. Some significant outcomes of her story were the development of ethics committees in hospitals, nursing homes, and hospices, and the introduction of advance health care directives. Karen Ann had ushered in a new realm of discourse and debate about the need to look more reasonably and compassionately at preserving comfort and dignity at life's end. In her tragic untimely dying, this young woman persuasively compels us to look into our heart and minds, to confront the inevitability of our own death. Sadly, she was not alone in this mission.

In 1983, just two years before Karen Ann was able to die, another young woman's life was about to change dramatically. Nancy Cruzan, a 25 year old woman in Missouri, was thrown from her car when it ran off the road and flipped over. Thrust into a persistent vegetative state, Nancy remained unchanged. After five years, her family was able to accept that their precious daughter would never improve. They then sadly embarked on a painful legal proceeding, seeking removal of her feeding tube to allow her to die. Tragically, she did not die until the day after Christmas, seven years later. A political cartoon sent to Nancy's family became her grave marker. It read: Born 7/20/57, Departed 1/11/83, At Peace 12/26/90. This sorrow-filled saga would continue.

In Florida, on Feb. 5th of the very same year Nancy died, Terri Schiavo, just twenty-six at the time and probably suffering from bulimia, collapsed at home from cardiac and respiratory arrest. While paramedics were able to restart her heart, Terri's brain had been without oxygen several minutes, causing her permanent brain damage. Unfortunately, Terri would not be allowed to die for fifteen more years—years fraught with failed rehabilitation attempts and diminishing hopes; with bitterness and family dissension as her husband Michael advocated for removal of Terri's feeding tubes while her parents steadfastly refused, maintaining that she was still conscious. The four years preceding the court's decision to at last permanently remove the feeding tube saw involvement by the pro-life movement, disability rights groups, members of the Florida legislature, the US Congress, and President George Bush himself. Tragically, Terri's case became a public spectacle. It should never have happened. Mercifully, she died in a Florida hospice on March 31, 2005.

Had these young women been able to discuss and clearly state in writing their end-of-life wishes, their agonizing scenarios—each lasting many years—would have played out very differently. Their families could have been spared much confusion, anguish, and heartache. Instead, costly legal struggles and disconcerting public scrutiny exhaustingly complicated what should have been a very private sorrow for each family.

Few of us would want to chance having these delicate, very personal decisions made by others. The *Living Will* and *Health Care Proxy* offer an opportunity to maintain control and make our own choices. The decisions we may make are ours and, if documented, can assure peace of mind, trusting our wishes will be honored.

Once again, how do we begin to define our wishes for our life's ending? Don't we all hope for a death that is peaceful and without regrets? You want to be in control, to be told the truth, to not be judged, to continue to be you. Ask yourself what would be most important to preserve at your life's ending? Why not reflect upon those things for which you are most hopeful (e.g., to be at home, near your family, with your pets) and, then, those things you may fear (e.g., pain, loss of dignity and control). Write them down! Perhaps they will be more easily dealt with if you can visualize your thoughts on paper or screen. Advance Care forms for your Living Will and Health Care Proxy are forms of documentation you can fill out as a way of making known your final wishes. Since forms may vary slightly from state to state, it will be wise to use those that are specific to your area.[2]

Your Living Will notes those life-supporting treatments you would favor or decline *only* if you were to be considered in an *irreversible* condition or could no longer express your wishes. Two words in the previous sentence must be emphasized. The first is *irreversible*. Of course, you would want every possible measure taken if there existed reasonable expectation for your recovery. The second word is *only*. Certainly, if you are able, you will express your wishes all along the way. Examples of treatments you may favor or decline would be CPR (cardiopulmonary resuscitation), blood transfusions, tube feedings, dialysis, and antibiotics.

2. There is, however, a form entitled "Five Wishes" that you may find especially helpful. Honored in 40 states, it has been called the first "living will with a heart." A user-friendly form, it can help to guide your family, doctors, and others involved in your care.

Very likely, you will desire to remain pain-free, clean, and comfortable. You would wish to be cared for with dignity and respect. You would hope to remain mentally clear and as alert as possible, enabling you to interact with your dear ones. And very likely, you will wish to be guided by your religious and personal beliefs so that you are at peace with your decisions.

It is also helpful and important to consider the influence of modern technology on your end-of-life choices. Medical advances have allowed extraordinary "miracles" to occur. In some circumstances, however, such interventions are no longer appropriate. They become efforts in futility, disrupting the natural progression of the dying process. Reflect carefully before you decide. And do be assured that your Living Will can be changed. Make sure your updated choices are clearly documented and that all copies reflect those changes.

A Health Care Proxy is a companion document and guide to a Living Will. It names that person, eighteen years or older, whom you have deemed responsible to communicate for you *only* if you are unable to make your own medical decisions. An alternate choice needs also to be named in the event your primary proxy is not available. Your choices for these important roles should not be taken lightly. The person(s) closest to you may not be the wisest choice. Such a person might consider the expectations of acting on your behalf to be too painful. Consider asking a trusted friend or associate who knows you well. You must be sure that your wishes will be respected and honored *even* if they are different from those held by your designees, for they may be. Candid and loving conversations will help you determine the best choice of proxies. You need to be able to know that they will speak *only* for you.

Another important point about these forms is that you *do not* need a lawyer to help you complete them. Also, be sure to give copies to your doctor, your proxy and alternate, and anyone else you feel should have one. Remember too to have a copy with you when traveling. Hopefully, it won't be needed, yet how considerate and illuminating if it should be.

Probably most important is to discuss these end-of-life issues with your dear ones. Not only can that enhance your own decision-making efforts, but it can also inspire others to do the same. It is a pity that such a small percentage of the population has done so. Immeasurable, unnecessary heartache would be spared if we all prepared these very important documents, dispensed them appropriately, and rested in the assurance they provide.

Truly, this preparation is a gift to our dear ones. So many families facing the impending death of a loved one have been in chaos trying to determine that person's final wishes. In what could be an intimate time of coming together, relationships can be strained, sometimes beyond repair. Oh! It could be so very different! Again, "preparing for death is one of the kindest and wisest things we can do for ourselves and others."

Death preparation has other dimensions worthy of our attention and, likewise, conducive to our peace of mind. What about planning your own funeral, this celebration of your life? Who better than you to choose your favorite readings and music, rather than have others wonder what those choices might be. Write them down. Funeral services, whatever their type, seem far more meaningful if they truly reflect the person they honor and remember.

I once knew a young man whose life was devoted to music. He also was dying. He met with his Pastor and, with infinite care, he laid out very specific detailed directions for his funeral Mass, selecting several of his favorite classical pieces. It was heavenly! He seemed so present to us all during that hour. It was a beautiful and quite unforgettable leave-taking. Another memorable funeral was that of a woman who, despite her blindness, had graciously and generously lived a life of service to others. I can still recall her funeral service when many soft smiles joined mine as, out of the silence, came the song she had requested, "Somewhere Over the Rainbow." It was a perfect ending, and we loved it. Of course, I have never forgotten it.

Your planning can go a step farther. Here again, several choices await as you consider the resting place of your body. How and where would you wish to be buried? If cremated, what about your ashes? Is there a favorite place you may wish to have them dispersed? Maybe you are interested in a "green burial." This option is offered in some communities. For a green burial, a body is wrapped in a simple shroud or a pine box and placed in the earth. Licensed funeral directors can offer knowledgeable guidance in all these matters, and many people have been grateful for this opportunity to pre-arrange their funerals, as are their families. As my sisters, brother, and I vigiled with our beloved Mom those final days and hours, the conversation quite naturally turned to her "arrangements." "Not to worry" I assured them. From her lovely old wooden bookcase with latticed windows, I withdrew a green folder. My mother and I had spent precious hours over a long period of time discussing, deciding, and noting preferences for her funeral and burial. Her arrangements were quite complete. Those hours, filled with both laughter and tears, will ever be a treasured memory.

There remains yet another aspect to your end-of-life reflection. How do you want to be remembered? What "gifts" will you leave those dear to you? While, of course, it is important that financial and legal matters be in order, may I suggest another type of will—that of your spirit. What are your beliefs, your hopes, your dreams? What is dearest to your heart? What is it that defines your personhood and how will you convey this to those you love? Remember, it will be those dear ones who will reflect the light of your life's candle.

Claudia, a lovely young mother of two small boys, graced Isaiah House in exquisite ways. Within days of her death, she welcomed to her bedside a cherished friend who offered to write the letters she would dictate. Her husband would keep them safely until the designated time. Such treasures for her dear children! The same day of the letter writing, Claudia's sister-in-law lovingly gave her a delicate hand-painted ceramic heart. It was to remain with us at Isaiah House after her death, a charming visual reminder of a remarkable young woman.

There are many ways to assure your legacy will live on. Audio and visual recordings preserve those precious voices, those smiles we never want to forget. Sharing favorite stories, family histories, the wisdom of your years will be so dearly appreciated, however you choose to do this. The ways of our leaving "parts" of ourselves will vary depending upon our experiences, interests, and talents. But oh, I urge you *not to wait*. Live in the now! Surely, when all is said and done, don't we hope not to be forgotten, to leave behind something of ourselves, to have made a difference?

A remarkable example is of my friend Rick, the last of my dying teachers about whom I will write. With gracious dignity, he faced the terrifying diagnosis of ALS ("Lou Gehrig's disease") and lived courageously—with his characteristic humor—for the next two years. The highlights of Rick's last Christmas were his gifts to his wife and two young sons. This is their story.

Far from being a sedentary soul, Rick had a passion for nature and many of the energetic activities invited by the outdoors. Running, hiking, climbing, and cycling were among his favorites. One can only imagine his heartbreaking acceptance of his body's gradual decline. Having participated in numerous running events, Rick had collected many T-shirts, each bearing the logo of that particular day's event. The shirts held stories waiting to be told. A dear friend of Rick, who was a quilter, fashioned three beautiful quilts, using the T-shirts. Each quilt also included carefully chosen photographs specifically for each loved one. The colorful quilts are a chronicle of their lives together. Each one holds its own memories and provided a life review for both Rick at that time and for his dear family for the remainder of their lives. With these most unique gifts, they will truly be wrapped in his love. Such a legacy—such a lesson. How will you be remembered? How would you hope to be remembered? In addition to the suggestions I have offered for preserving presence and memories, know that the way we live each day also becomes part of our legacy.

Earlier, I wrote about the painful impact of our re-grets. We all have things we haven't said, done, or finished. Yet those regrets could be minimized along the way if we chose to live in the moment, not procrastinate, and always follow our heart's nudges. Accepting the reality that each day might be our last, which it well could be, can prompt us to respond to life with vitality, recognizing fully the gift it truly is.

For as long as I can recall, I have enjoyed making lists of tasks needing my attention. Their content, of course, changes with the task, but it is such a delight to cross out the items, one by one. Several years ago, I became aware of an addition I was making to the headings of my various lists—the word "hopefully." Was that perhaps reflecting my deepening awareness of life's fragility, its ability to change in a moment, sometimes in a devastating way? How can we just assume that one breath will follow another—and another; that we'll wake up each morning and then see days ending? Shouldn't our first thought upon awakening be one of gratitude—because there are many for whom a new day does not arrive. Is not each birthday a "gift day"? For surely it is just that. This mindfulness of the moment, rather than dampening our spirit, should well serve to heighten and enliven our sensibilities. Once again, *carpe diem*—seize the day. You will never have it again.

* * *

With many others deeply committed to the philosophy of hospice and the blessings of a natural death, I have often wondered if we might be able to make a difference in the way many Americans view death. End-of-life choices can be, and often are, agonizingly painful. Our technologies have quite a hold on us: "Is there another treatment we can try?" Sometimes we simply don't know when to stop. Many people have heard frightening stories or had negative personal experiences around death, and these can color views of what it may be like. Lacking awareness of the dying process and how to get through it, many families find themselves desperately seeking guidance and reassurance. These, and many other issues surrounding end-of-life, can be complex and controversial. In the midst of all this bewilderment, might it be possible to make a difference? Many impassioned conversations have led to just one conclusion—Yes it is possible! But how? The only answer is to educate.

There are many perspectives from which one might begin to enlighten minds and hearts and, certainly, each writer has her own. For me, it has been the lovely old house named Isaiah and *all* the dear hearts within. Their living, their dying have graced my life abundantly. May their stories have done the same for you—even in some small way. Blessings!

"If you learn not to be afraid of your own death, then you realize that you do not need to fear anything else either."[3]

—John O'Donohue

3. O'Donohue, *Anam Cara*, 218.

Bibliography

Blaze, Penny. "You Must Get Over It!!!." Compassionate Friends Brisbane Newsletter (June/July 2007). Accessed March 13, 2011. http://www.uq.net.au/tcfbrisbane/JunJul07.htm#Item%204.

Gregory, David, and John English. "The Myth of Control: Suffering in Palliative Care." *Journal of Palliative Care* 10 (1994) 18–22.

Gyatso, Geshe Kelsang. dealingwithfear.org. Accessed March 13, 2011. http://www.dealingwithfear.org/fear-of-death.htm/.

Lane, Julia. "Care of the Human Spirit." *Journal of Professional Nursing* 3 (1987) 332–37.

Moore, Thomas. "Growing through Grief." *Spirituality and Health* (January/February 2007). Accessed March 11, 2011. http://www.spiritualityhealth.com/NMagazine/articles.php?id=1646.

Nouwen, Henry, Donald P. McNeill, and Douglas A. Morrison. *Compassion: A Reflection on the Christian Life.* New York: Image Books Doubleday, 1982.

O'Donohue, John. *Anam Cara: A Book of Celtic Wisdom.* New York: Clift Street Books, 1997.

Poer, Nancy. *Living into Dying: A Journal of Spiritual and Practical Death Care for Family and Community.* Philomath, OR: Waldorf Books, 2002.

Saunders, Cicely. "Care of the Dying: The Problem of Euthanasia." Nursing Times 72 (1976) 1003–5.

Steere, Douglas V. *Gleanings: A Random Harvest.* Nashville: Upper Room, 1986.

The Northumbria Community. "Walking With Grief." In *Celtic Daily Prayers and Readings from the Northumbria Community.* New York: HarperOne, 2002.

Wiederkehr, Macrina. *Seasons of Your Heart: Prayers and Reflection.* San Francisco: HarperOne, 1991.